LONDON
THE PANORAMAS

LONDON

THE PANORAMAS

MARK DENTON

CONSTABLE · LONDON

Constable & Robinson
3 The Lanchesters
162 Fulham Palace Road
London W6 9ER
www.constablerobinson.com

First published in the UK in 2006 by Constable, an imprint of Constable & Robinson Ltd

A copy of the British Library Cataloguing in Publication Data is available from the British Library.

ISBN-13 978-1-84529-273-7
ISBN-10 1-84529-273-1

10 8 6 4 2   3 5 7 9

DUCK FLOTILLA, SERPENTINE, HYDE PARK

CONTENTS

LONDON EYE AT NIGHT

INTRODUCTION

London is a city of panoramas – geographical, social, and historical. Europe's largest conurbation covers 600 square miles (1,555 sq km) and is home to over eight million people, speaking around 300 different languages. A far cry from the day in AD43 when the Romans founded a storage depot on the marshy banks of the Thames and called it Londinium.

London gained pre-eminence among English cities when William the Conqueror became the first king of England to be crowned in Westminster Abbey, on Christmas Day 1066. Soon after, William built the White Tower that is now the centrepiece of the Tower of London, cementing his dominance over the merchants who made London one of Europe's most powerful cities during the following centuries. Fire, however, respects nothing, and much of the medieval and Tudor city went up in flames during the Great Fire of London in 1666. More than 13,000 buildings, including 90 churches, were destroyed – ending a cycle of devastation begun the year before when the Great Plague decimated the city's population.

Then as now, London's energy spurred on a reinvention of the city, under the guidance of the architect Sir Christopher Wren, whose St Paul's Cathedral proved just one of many key buildings. Another burst of building during the 19th century reflected London's role as hub of a British Empire spanning the globe. The bombs of Hitler's Luftwaffe wrought fresh havoc on the city during the Second World War, and in the years after the war swathes of mediocre architecture were thrown up as an impoverished and exhausted Britain struggled to rebuild its capital. Since the 1980s, though, London has begun to show renewed care for its architectural character, with a string of iconic buildings providing points of focus – the London Eye (better known as The Wheel), Tate Modern, the new Wembley Stadium, a remodelled South Bank Centre, plus plans for a revamped Battersea Power Station.

Throughout its history, London has maintained an antipathy towards the sort of planning that moulded cities such as Paris, with its elegant 19th-century boulevards and architectural styles imposed by Hausmann, or the formal grid of numbered avenues that cut between New York's forest of skyscrapers. Instead London is bonded together with the help of its villages. Unlike American cities with their clear divisions into downtown and suburbia, London's heart – the City of London and the West End – is complemented by outlying former villages gradually absorbed by the city's sprawl, while still maintaining their own identity and structure. Hampstead in the north, Blackheath to the south-east and Richmond in the west are just three which feature in the following pages.

To truly get a feel for London, therefore, visitors should go beyond the most familiar places on the tourist map. London is much more than the West End. So, as well as Covent Garden market, visit Brick Lane and Spitalfield in the East End. In search of historic houses, look farther than Buckingham Palace to discover the marvellous Elizabethan-meets-Art Deco hideaway that is Eltham Palace. Skip the over-priced West End bars to sample the eclectic watering holes of Hoxton. The same need to explore applies in the centre of the city, too. There's a local saying that tourists walk along Oxford Street, while Londoners cut across it, heading into Soho to the south or Fitzrovia to the north.

Around 700 of the city's buildings bear blue plaques (www.blueplaque.com) informing you of famous past occupants. There's even one for the fictional detective Sherlock Holmes at 221b Baker Street. For London's people are as much a part of its character and appeal as its historic buildings, wonderful shops or beautiful parks. London is the most cosmopolitan city in Europe, extending a welcome from the Huguenots, who fled persecution in 17th-century France, to the global diaspora that add to the city's colour and vitality today. All around London, certain areas take on the flavour of specific communities – Portuguese around Vauxhall, Caribbean in Brixton, Jewish in Golders Green, Bangladeshi in Brick Lane.

Like the city's architecture, variety triumphs over homogeneity in its population. Tolerance is a London trademark – a crucial one with so many people crammed so close together. What may be branded English aloofness is often simply a respect for privacy in a city where space, both physical and personal, can sometimes be at a premium. But don't be fooled. London is a friendly city as well as a big one: expansive in every sense.

WESTMINSTER AND THE WEST END

Like the Eiffel Tower in Paris, the London Eye – usually just The Wheel to Londoners – was intended to be a temporary structure. London, like Paris, saw sense, leaving The Wheel to imprint its beautiful circle on the rectangular urban skyline.

Across the river, the famous honey-coloured stones of the Palace of Westminster have stood for nearly a thousand years. The mother of parliaments is one of London's most famous icons – almost as familiar as the sound of Big Ben which marks the passing of the day across London and, via BBC radio, across the world. Big Ben, of course, is the name of the bell not the clock tower, and you can see where the world's most famous chime was born by taking a Saturday tour of the Whitechapel Bell Foundry. Founded in 1570 and still at work today, it's one of the oldest companies in the world, forging not only Big Ben (1858) but also the original of America's famous Liberty Bell (1752).

Back by the Thames, in the shadow of The Wheel, the grand County Hall building was once home to London's left wing Greater London Council. It languished empty for years after Prime Minister Margaret Thatcher abolished the GLC in 1986, until rescued by advertising guru Charles Saatchi to house his famous collection of modern art. The old wood-panelled rooms provide a striking backdrop for controversial works such as Damien Hirst's dead shark floating in its huge tank of formaldehyde.

While the Victoria Embankment running along the north bank of the Thames cries out for a

AVENUE, GREEN PARK

purpose other than the snarl of traffic, Trafalgar Square a few hundred yards to the north-west is an example of London renewing a key space to great effect. For decades, this magnificent square was reduced to little more than a giant roundabout. Nelson's Column, a towering monument to England's greatest admiral, and Edward Landseer's magnificent bronze lions brooded over a pigeon-filled space which came alive only for occasional protest rallies and as a rowdy gathering place on New Year's Eve.

The return of a London-wide council in 2000 – led by the former head of the old GLC Ken Livingstone – has seen Trafalgar Square reborn as a place for people rather than cars. A sweeping expanse of white stone now frames the twin buildings of the National Gallery – the 1820s original and the modern Sainsbury Wing, famously denounced by Prince Charles in 1991 as 'a monstrous carbuncle on the face of a much-loved and elegant friend'! In the square's north-west corner is the Fourth Plinth, site for a rotating series of sculptures which kicked off with Marc Quinn's statue depicting artist Alison Lapper, born without arms or feet, when eight months pregnant. Always happy to indulge in vociferous public debate, many Londoners criticised the work's position alongside more traditional statues but others praised it as a concrete manifestation of London's tolerance of difference.

London's parks, of course, welcome everyone. Green Park is the largest of the city's central parks, bordering Piccadilly with its famous hotels such as The Ritz, and luxury shopping spots such as Burlington Arcade and the Royal Academy art gallery. First recorded in 1554, Green Park's name refers to its relative lack of flowers. For its first two centuries, it was best known as the site of frequent duels rather than relaxation. Though now devoid of buildings, the Park once contained a Temple of Peace and a Temple of Concord, both destroyed during firework displays – the former in 1749, the latter in 1814. The park was opened to the public in 1826.

For many Londoners, though, St James Park has a greater appeal despite its small size of 54 acres (22 hectares). The oldest of the city's Royal Parks, it is surrounded by three palaces – Westminster (Parliament), St James's Palace and Buckingham Palace, the latter at the end of arguably London's most beautiful stretch of road, The Mall. Once a marshy water meadow, St James's Park took its name from a leper hospital founded here in the 13th century. In 1532 Henry VIII acquired the site to satisfy his passion for hunting, and built the Palace of St James. Elizabeth I used the park for frequent fetes, though it had a more sordid reputation as a meeting place for sexual encounters, chronicled by the rakish aristocrat John Wilmot, the Earl of Rochester – subject of the 2005 film The Libertine.

Horse Guards Parade stands on the east side of the park, home to the Queen's traditional corps of soldiers, within a short horse ride from the monarch's famous residence at the western end of the Mall. Outside Buckingham Palace is the Queen Victoria Memorial, including not only a statue of England's longest-reigning monarch but also figures of Victory, Courage and Constancy, and ornamental gates given by three of Britain's former Dominions – Australia, South Africa and Canada.

VIEW EAST, PARK LANE HILTON

MORNING SUNSHINE, PALACE OF WESTMINSTER

TRAFFIC TRAILS, PICCADILLY CIRCUS

DAWN, ST JAMES'S PARK

MORNING DASH, VICTORIA EMBANKMENT

NARNIA LAMPS, GREEN PARK

TATTERSHALL CASTLE AND WESTMINSTER FROM THAMES

WINTER TREE, BIG BEN

LONE SWAN, ST JAMES'S PARK

CRESCENT MOON AT DAWN, THAMES

FLOWER BEDS, GREEN PARK GATE

WESTMINSTER ABBEY AT NIGHT

VICTORIA EMBANKMENT, DAWN

PALACE OF WESTMINSTER AND THE THAMES

TRAFALGAR SQUARE BY NIGHT

BUCKINGHAM PALACE FROM ST JAMES'S PARK

BIG BEN AND TRAFFIC TRAILS

THE CITY AND DOCKLANDS

Before stretching its urban tentacles to become Europe's most sprawling metropolis, London was the City and the docks – the latter providing the conduit for a vast global trade, the former turning the ensuing wealth into architectural grandeur. The City's ancient taverns and coffee houses also provided the setting for artistic endeavours, frequented by the likes of Samuel Pepys and William Shakespeare.

London Bridge was originally the only crossing over the Thames. The bridge went through various incarnations, one of the more recent of which was later bought by a American, believing he was buying the famous Tower Bridge (he made the best of his mistake by erecting his bridge on the Colorado River south of Las Vegas). As London expanded more bridges were added, but all were to the west of London Bridge, since the river to the east needed free flow of shipping as the hub of one of the world's busiest ports.

By the mid-1800s, the east end of London had become so densely populated that public pressure mounted for a bridge east of London Bridge, since road journeys for east Londoners to the south side of the Thames were taking hours. Over 50 designs were put forward to build a bridge which wouldn't disrupt river traffic, but it was several years before a design by Horace Jones provided the solution in the shape of Tower Bridge, the superbly engineered drawbridge still in operation today.

While historic buildings remain throughout the City of London, many became surrounded by nondescript architecture as London grew careless of its beautiful heritage. Views of St Paul's Cathedral – built by Sir Christopher Wren in the 1660s – became a particular battleground, with increasing protests over buildings that might obstruct sightlines of this iconic landmark. The building of the Millennium Bridge was a breakthrough in the campaign for a more thoughtful attitude to London's appearance. This graceful structure was not only the first new Thames crossing since the completion of Tower Bridge in 1894, but also a victory for those keen to open up London to the admiring gaze. The bridge creates a breathtaking sightline connecting St Paul's with the equally striking Tate Modern art gallery.

The most recent masterpiece to appear on the City skyline is the Swiss Re building – whose shape earned it the immediate nickname of 'The Gherkin'. Located at 30 St Mary's Axe (characterful old street names are a pleasure of any City walk), this 40-storey beauty is often credited to architect Sir Norman Foster but the original design was by Foster's then-associate Ken Shuttleworth – the architect also behind the Millennium Bridge and the giant arches of the new Wembley Stadium (see Bloomsbury And To The North). Its very existence is an example of recycling, using land created by the demolition of the Baltic Exchange that stood here until damaged beyond repair by an IRA terrorist bomb in 1992.

Two decades before 'The Gherkin', another iconic skyscraper emerged on the London skyline. Rather than appearing in the heart of the City, the Canary Wharf skyscraper rose above the derelict docks of Isle of Dogs – a regenerative move that is typical of London's ongoing desire for reinvention. This beautiful building echoed New York's finest with its clean-lined silvery Art Deco styling. For years it stood proudly alone as the major landmark on the east London skyline, surrounded by patches of water on which old boats and machinery were left as mementoes of past industrial glory.

A sudden spurt of building in the last decade has seen the Canary Wharf Tower joined by a series of companion skyscrapers. For an overview of the changes transforming Docklands and the east of London – even more so after London's successful bid for the 2012 Olympics – take a trip on the Docklands Light Railway (DLR), whose driverless trains whisk passengers on a computer-controlled journey from the heart of the City to the eastern edge of the former docks.

Back in the City, some things are being left as they were. Leadenhall Market – named after a lead-roofed mansion that stood nearby in the 14th century – is built on the site of a Roman forum, and has been a food market since the Middle Ages. The present building is Victorian, built in 1881 by architect Horace Jones, who also found time to design two of London's other famous food markets, Billingsgate and Smithfield, as well as Tower Bridge. A visit to this trio of City markets would start with early morning fish (6-8am, not Monday) at Billingsgate, moving on to meat at Smithfield (perhaps pausing for one of the famously filling breakfasts available at the morning pubs in the area) and ending with lunch at Leadenhall. A real taste of London life, in every sense.

DYING SUN FROM TOWER 42

LEADENHALL MARKET

RAINBOW, TOWER BRIDGE

CHINESE BARGE, CANARY WHARF

ROYAL VICTORIA DOCK AT DAWN

MILLENNIUM BRIDGE AT NIGHT

VIEW EAST FROM THE MONUMENT

EVENING, LIMEHOUSE BASIN

ROYAL EXCHANGE, THE CITY

ST PAUL'S CATHEDRAL

NEW CITY FROM EAST INDIA

VIEW FROM TATE MODERN BALCONY

ST PAUL'S FROM MILLENNIUM BRIDGE

MILLENNIUM MILL, ROYAL VICTORIA DOCK

CANARY WHARF FIREWORKS

BLOOMSBURY AND TO THE NORTH

To any well-read Londoner, the mention of Bloomsbury immediately conjures up the names of the Bloomsbury Set – most famously, novelist Virginia Woolf and painters Vanessa Bell and Duncan Grant – who took up residence in this neighbourhood just north of the West End in the years before the First World War. Today Bloomsbury remains a centre of learning – from the vast British Museum (the world's first major public museum when founded in 1759 and still one of its finest) to the London colleges clustered around Russell Square. A little further out, the chichi lanes of Hampstead, the streets around Regent's Park and the pretty waterways of Little Venice are home to many of London's creative A-list.

As befits an area where thoughtful wandering is in order, this slice of north London has its share of green spaces, of which the 800-acre (325-hectare) Hampstead Heath is the most beautiful. First recorded in 1312, this former area of rough moorland supplied firewood to London for centuries, as well as water. The heath is still famous for its 25 ponds, some of which provide London's most characterful places to swim.

LAMPS, ALEXANDRA PALACE

Hampstead Heath's most famous building is Kenwood House, built in the early 1600s but remodelled in the 18th century by architect Robert Adam. For over half a century, classical concerts have been held by the lake in its formal gardens, attracting thousands of people each summer. Beside the heath, Parliament Hill was dubbed Traitors Hill when it became a meeting place for troops loyal to Parliament during the English Civil War. Now it is a mecca for kite flyers, as well as offering one of the finest views of London.

Also built on an elevated position is Alexandra Palace. Despite its name, it has nothing to do with royalty. Sited on the highest point of Muswell Hill in 1873, it was intended to be a 'People's Palace', a place of entertainment to rival the Crystal Palace (see Hyde Park To Hampton Court). Nicknamed 'Ally Pally', it also became the location of the world's first public TV service in 1936 when the BBC began broadcasting from here.

While Alexandra Palace's star has faded, the 487-acre (200-hectare) Regent's Park remains a magnet for Londoners in search of entertainment – a popular place to play various sports, as well as home to both London Zoo and the city's Open Air Theatre with its summer stagings of Shakespeare. Three sides of the park are lined with elegant white terraces of houses designed by John Nash. The park also contains several villas, of which the most prominent is the Marquis of Hertford's Villa, rebuilt as Winfield House in the 1930s and now the American Ambassador's residence.

Running through the northern end of the park, Regent's Canal was once a major trade route connecting the Grand Union Canal from the north of England with the former London Docks. You can still walk along the canal from Little Venice in the north to the Limehouse Basin in the east, pausing perhaps at the London Canal Museum in King's Cross or at Camden Lock market.

Two other icons of London feature in this chapter, both legacies of the Swinging Sixties. The BT Tower – known as the Post Office Tower when it opened in 1964 to the north of Oxford Street in the West End – was the place to get a panorama of London long before the London Eye rose on the south bank of the Thames. A futuristic symbol of a resurgent Britain, it came with a restaurant and cocktail bar 500 feet (150 metres) up. The tower, alas, closed to the public in 1980.

Another London icon which enjoyed its finest hour in the 1960s was Wembley Stadium. Originally known as the Empire Stadium, Brazilian superstar Pele called it the 'church of football'. Built for the British Empire Exhibition of 1924, its famous 'Twin Towers' hosted England's international matches, five European Cup finals, and each season's final of the FA Cup. Now, a 21st-century Wembley is nearing completion. Designed by Ken Shuttleworth – the architect behind two other London landmarks, the Millennium Bridge and the Swiss Re building – the new stadium replaces the former building's twins towers with a soaring arch. As London looks to a bright future, the new Wembley will play its role as a venue for matches in the 2012 Olympic Games.

EVENING SKIES FROM PRIMROSE HILL

LEAVES, RUSSELL SQUARE

CRANES, NEW WEMBLEY STADIUM

DAWN COLOURS, LITTLE VENICE

BANDSTAND IN WINTER, REGENT'S PARK

GARY CLIMBS THE WRITER, PARLIAMENT HILL

COLONNADE, REGENT'S CRESCENT

BT TOWER FROM REGENT'S PARK

SUMMER, HAMPSTEAD HEATH

KENWOOD HOUSE, HAMPSTEAD HEATH

LAMPS, ALEXANDRA PALACE

AUTUMN, TAVISTOCK SQUARE

BT TOWER FROM CAPPER STREET

SWANS, HAMPSTEAD HEATH

CRACKED ICE, REGENT'S PARK

H Y D E   P A R K   T O   H A M P T O N   C O U R T

The Thames may flow east towards its appointment with the North Sea but London's money has traditionally flowed the other way. For centuries, financial and trading fortunes made in the City of London or its dockland quays took on luxurious form in the west – from the present day wealthy trendsetters of Notting Hill to the historic palaces at Richmond, Kensington and Hampton Court.

West London is bookmarked by two of the city's great parks. Hyde Park, with its famous lake The Serpentine (created in the 1730s by Queen Caroline, wife of George II), marks the edge of the West End shopping district, while Richmond Park marks the western edge of London itself.

Covering 350 acres (140 hectares), Hyde Park was owned by the monks of Westminster Abbey until 1536 when it was acquired by Henry VIII as a private hunting ground. Charles I opened the park to the public in 1637, and two decades later it became a sanctuary for thousands fleeing the Great Plague that struck the City of London in 1665. The park remains a sanctuary today from the traffic thundering past the imposing Marble Arch, moved to the park's north-east corner from Buckingham Palace in 1851. Hyde Park also possesses its own Royal palace. Kensington Palace became home to the court of William III towards the end of the 17th century, and was later the birthplace and childhood home of Queen Victoria. But it is best known today as the home of the late Princess Diana, killed in a car crash in 1997.

Hyde Park was the site of Britain's first artificially lit highway when William III installed 300 oil lamps along the route now bearing the evocative name Rotten Row – a corruption of the French 'Route de Roi' (King's Road) rather than anything unpleasant. The park has also hosted major celebrations since 1814 when fireworks marked the end of the Napoleonic Wars. During the Great Exhibition of 1851 the famous iron-and-glass Crystal Palace was built here before being moved to south London, where it burned down in 1936. More recently, rock concerts have brought vast crowds to the park, from the legendary 1969 free concert by the Rolling Stones to the Live 8 show of 2005.

Mementoes of Queen Victoria's consort Prince Albert imprint the landscape as you move west. The Albert Memorial, unveiled by Victoria in 1876 following Albert's death from typhoid aged just 42, though its array of marble testaments to industry, the arts and the world's continents, mark it as a monument to a global Empire as much as to the memory of one man. A few hundred yards away, the soaring dome of the Albert Hall encloses a unique circular auditorium which is one of London's major music spaces. The hall's annual 'Proms' classical concerts are as much part of London's summer social calendar as Wimbledon or the Chelsea Flower Show.

Head south, past Harrods and a cluster of London's great museums – the Victoria & Albert, Natural History Museum and Science Museum – and you come to the Albert Bridge. Opened in 1873, the bridge was almost demolished after the Second World War because of structural problems. Though strengthened, it still bears wartime signs telling soldiers from nearby Chelsea Barracks to break step when marching over it in case vibrations caused a collapse!

West along the riverbank you pass the houses of London's super-rich – from luxury houseboats to Marble Hill House, the Palladian villa built in the 1720s for Henrietta Howard, mistress of George II, where she entertained not only her royal lover but also great writers of the day such as Jonathan Swift.

The western edge of London comes at Richmond Park. London's largest Royal Park (2,500 acres/1,010 hectares) is also its most wild, a designated nature reserve whose ancient woods and grassland have changed little since its foundation in the 13th century. The park's deer were introduced by Charles I in the early 1620s when he moved his court to Richmond Palace to escape plague in the city. Today Richmond offers a feel of the countryside while still having a view of St Paul's Cathedral, 12 miles (19 kilometres) to the east.

Nearby is London's most famous Victorian greenhouse, the Palm House in Kew Gardens. The gardens themselves were created as a pleasure garden for Prince Frederick in 1731, becoming the Royal Botanic Gardens in 1759. Some of the earliest of its 50,000 botanical specimens were brought back by Captain Cook from his famous Pacific voyages. Built in the 1840s, the Palm House is one of London's most recognisable structures (as well as a warm sanctuary on a winter's day). Built using techniques developed from shipbuilding, the building has been compared to the upturned hull of a graceful ocean liner. Kew can be reached by river – a cruise from Westminster Pier takes just over an hour.

VIEW WEST, PARK LANE HILTON

STREAM, RICHMOND PARK

FLUFFY CLOUD, HAMPTON COURT PALACE

LEAF SHOWER, KEW

HOUSEBOATS, KEW BRIDGE

SERPENTINE SUNSET, HYDE PARK

TEMPLE, KEW GARDENS

KENSINGTON GORE AND ROYAL ALBERT HALL

MARBLE HILL HOUSE, RIVER THAMES

BLUE DUSK, ALBERT BRIDGE

HORSECHESTNUT, THAMES PATH

PALM HOUSE, KEW GARDENS

ALBERT MEMORIAL, HYDE PARK

LAKE AT KEW GARDENS

ROYAL ALBERT HALL, AFTERNOON SUN

GARDENS, KENSINGTON PALACE

AUTUMN TREES, RICHMOND PARK

VIEW FROM HENRY VIII'S MOUND, RICHMOND PARK

THE SOUTH BANK

Since London's foundation in Roman times, the Thames has loomed large in the city's daily life – a major thoroughfare as well as the conduit for the maritime trade that brought London prosperity. Sad then, that London has rather turned its back on the river, with pleasure boats making up most of the Thames' traffic rather than river buses whisking Londoners quickly up and downstream as they once did.

The river frontage on the south side puts the north bank and its soulless swirl of traffic to shame. Things begin just east of Westminster Bridge and The Wheel with Europe's largest arts complex – the National Theatre, Royal Festival Hall, Queen Elizabeth Hall, Purcell Room, Hayward Gallery and National Film Theatre. Only the Royal Festival Hall survives from the original South Bank complex built in the wake of the 1951 Festival of Britain, and its elegant glass-fronted curves inspire an affection in marked contrast to attitudes towards the grey concrete 'Brutalist' style of the other buildings that followed in the 1960s. Thankfully, a radical landscaping and greening of the South Bank site is under way, which may finally make Londoners love it as a whole.

Moving east, Coin Street and the Oxo Tower offer a mix of design shops and restaurants, complemented a mile or so further downstream by the Design Museum, housed in a modernist riverside building just past London Bridge. Historic ships punctuate the walk along the south bank. A reconstruction of Sir Francis Drake's Tudor flagship the Golden Hinde sits in a tiny dock near St Mary Overie church. On the other side of London Bridge, HMS Belfast is a huge sleek memento of Britain's Second World War navy, playing a key role in the destruction of the German battleship *Scharnhorst* as well as in the Normandy landings.

Between the two ships, Borough Market is a colourful rendezvous (best on Friday and Saturday mornings) for anyone in search of good food or people-watching from the market's neighbouring cafes and restaurants. Next, downstream from the Design Museum, a modern glass building in the shape of a giant headlamp is home of the city's governing body, the Greater London Authority.

Keep on, past a mix of old housing and rusting riverbank mementoes of London's past, and the soaring masts of the *Cutty Sark* loom above Greenwich. Built in 1869, this beautiful ship was one of the fastest sailing vessels ever built, speeding tea from China and wool from Australia to London in record times until retired in 1922. The nearby Royal Naval College is one of the finest buildings in London, built on the site of the Tudor palace where Henry VIII was born, by two of Britain's finest architects, Sir Christopher Wren and his pupil Nicholas Hawksmoor.

Rising behind the college, Greenwich Park offers superb views of the city. Landscaped in 1662 by André le Nôtre, the designer of the legendary gardens at Versailles, the park boasts several historic buildings – the National Maritime Museum, the Ranger's House (with its fine collection of musical instruments) and the Queen's House. The latter was built by Inigo Jones for the wife of James I – though tragically she died before it was finished. The Greenwich Observatory, meanwhile, is the place from which the world's time (Greenwich Meantime or GMT) is measured. This is the place where, by standing astride the meridian line, visitors can say they have a foot in two different hemispheres.

Blackheath, to the south of Greenwich, is one of London's most historic open spaces – a rallying point in 1381 when Wat Tyler's peasant army almost overthrew King Richard II, and the place where Henry V was greeted on his return from the famous victory at Agincourt in 1415. Bordered by the pretty streets of Blackheath Village, the heath is now a rival to Parliament Hill in north London as the city's kite-flying mecca.

Dinosaurs stalk the undergrowth as you sweep through south-east London to Crystal Palace Park. These full-sized stone models were created during the 19th century by Benjamin Watkins, a testament to the Victorian obsession with paleontology as well as a complement to the Crystal Palace that was moved here from Hyde Park (and later burned down in 1936). The park is also home to one of London's few mazes.

A westward arc brings us back to the river via Battersea – home to Britain's most famous dog sanctuary, a pleasant Victorian park whose Pagoda is one of the more unusual landmarks on the Thames, and Battersea Power Station. Its quartet of giant chimneys make the power station one of London's most recognisable buildings (even more so after it featured on the cover of Pink Floyd's *Animals* album), and its fate is a symbol of the city's recent history – closed by Margaret Thatcher's government, it may now finally be regenerated by plans to turn it into a giant entertainment complex.

STORMY AFTERNOON, LONDON EYE

BATTERSEA POWER STATION

MILLENNIUM DOME AT DAWN

APRIL BLOSSOM AND CANARY WHARF, FROM GREENWICH PARK

NATIONAL THEATRE AT NIGHT

LAMP AND LONDON EYE

GREENWICH YACHT CLUB

TELEVISION MAST, CRYSTAL PALACE

FIREWORKS IN BATTERSEA PARK, ACROSS THE THAMES

ROYAL NAVAL COLLEGE, GREENWICH

DINOSAUR LAKE, CRYSTAL PALACE PARK

FIERY DAWN, JUBILEE BRIDGE

THE PARAGON, BLACKHEATH

DAWN FROM WATERLOO BRIDGE

CLOUD BANKS FROM GREENWICH PARK

LOOKING EAST, LONDON EYE

CUTTY SARK, SPRING MORNING

CHRISTMAS LIGHTS, SOUTH BANK

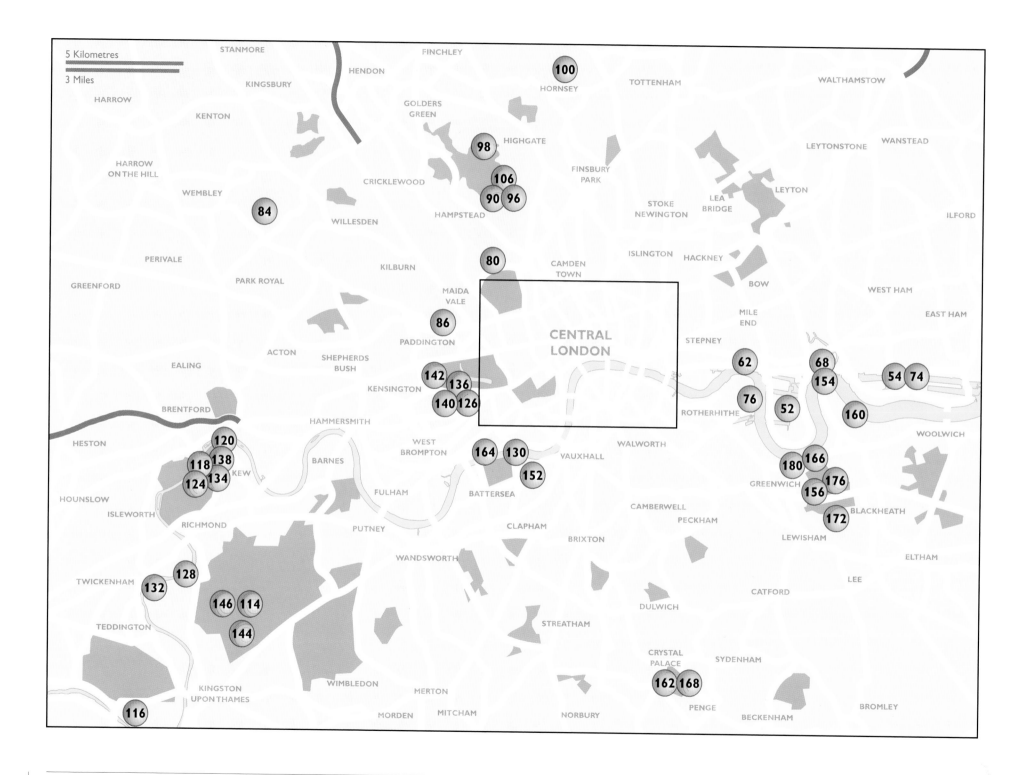

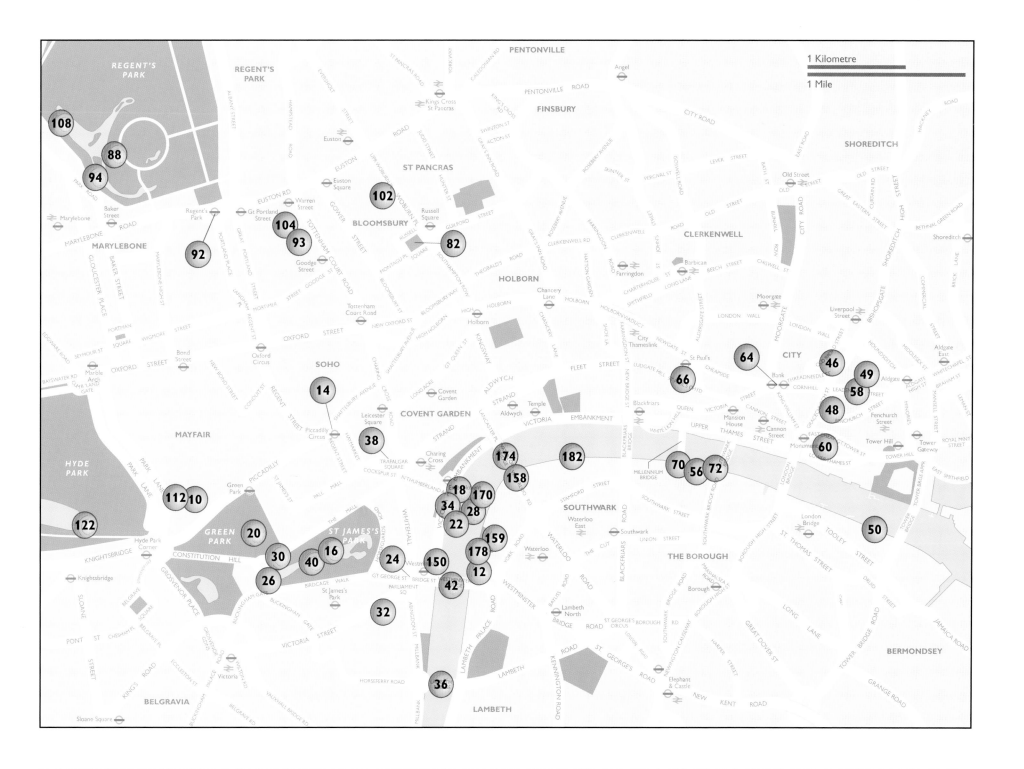

NOTES ON THE PHOTOGRAPHS

I principally employed two panoramic film cameras, the Fuji G617 and Fotoman 617; 617 refers to the size of the image captured on the film, which is roughly 6 x17 cm, or more precisely 4 exposures of 56 x 168 mm on 120 roll film. This is around 11 times the size of a 35mm slide and consequently delivers fantastic image quality.

I had been using the Fuji camera extensively for a couple of years when I began shooting in London, and despite rough treatment it has always given fine results with its fixed 105mm Fujinon lens. However, for this project I was also asked to test-drive a new 617 camera from a small Hong Kong-based outfit called Fotoman. I used it with a 180mm Rodenstock lens and a ground glass to aid composition. The Fotoman necessitated a more painstaking approach to my work when compared to the Fuji – it is no SLR where you can see through the lens, and the viewfinders supplied become less accurate as the focal length increases – but the results are worth the extra effort.

Balancing light is the principal technical concern when I am shooting landscapes. The slide film I most often used, Fuji Velvia, is highly sensitive and will easily burn out or black out if improperly exposed. To get the best results I measure light with a Pentax Digital Spotmeter, and then use Lee neutral density filters to balance areas of light and shadow.

pages 10-11
View east, Park Lane Hilton
Nov 2005; Fuji G617 105mm, Lee 0.6 ND grad, Velvia 50 asa
A small residue of violet earth shadow hangs over central London on a cool November evening. This view from the top floor of the Park Lane Hilton compacts many landmarks into a curiously small channel, but what I particularly noticed were the trees of Green Park defiantly holding their leaves despite the impending winter.

pages 12-13
Morning sunshine, Palace of Westminster
Jan 2006; Fotoman 617 180mm Rodenstock, Lee 0.6 ND grad, Velvia 50 asa
A sparkling winter morning on the South Bank. Curiously, the speeding barge totally escaped my attention, displaced by two policemen approaching from my left. From a distance, the 180mm lens on the Fotoman could pass for a rocket launcher, so it was unsurprising that they had to investigate.

pages 14-15
Traffic trails, Piccadilly Circus
Sept 2005; Fuji G617 105mm, Lee 0.9 ND grad, Velvia 50 asa
Piccadilly Circus was a subject that I was quietly dreading given the crowds that besiege it at all hours of the day. After an extended period of scouting I positioned myself near the traffic lights for a 30-second exposure, and was cheered by a passing cabbie stopping there. 'That's a big camera,' he remarked, not unreasonably.

pages 16-17
Dawn, St James's Park
Sept 2005; Fuji G617 105mm, Lee 0.6 ND grad & polarizer, Velvia 50 asa
The bridge view in St James's is one of the most famous in the capital, but it didn't seem that dawn was the ideal time to shoot it, with strong sunlight coming from behind Horse Guards Parade. Use of a polarizer and an angled grad made all the difference, giving strong colour and pleasing skies.

pages 18-19
Morning dash, Victoria Embankment
Jan 2006; Fuji G617 105mm, Lee 0.6 ND grad, Velvia 50 asa
The early morning race of expensive vehicles on the Embankment contrasted harshly with the homeless sleeping on the stairs and in the lift of Jubilee Bridge. Falling somewhere between the two states of urgently needing to be somewhere and having nowhere to go at all, I felt the most fortunate.

pages 20-21
Narnia lamps, Green Park
Oct 2005; Fotoman 617 180mm Rodenstock, Lee 81d, Velvia 50 asa
I hadn't expected to find inspiration in Green Park, given the lack of lakes and notable monuments, but I was immediately struck by the elegant avenues and ornate lighting. The image was taken shortly after dawn and f32 was used to lengthen the exposure to 25 seconds, removing any trace of the suited procession marching to work.

pages 22-23
Tattershall Castle and Westminster
Jan 2006; Fotoman 617 180mm Rodenstock unfiltered, Fuji RTP 64
The paddle steamer *Tattershall Castle* once ferried passengers across the River Humber. Saved from the breaker's yard, it now serves as a riverside bar, facing the Palace of Westminster. These sightlines proved irresistible, and the foreshortening effect of the 180mm lens helped to stress its wonderful location.

pages 24-25
Winter tree, Big Ben
Apr 2005; Fuji G617 105mm, Lee 0.6 ND grad & polarizer, Velvia 50 asa
Here a polarizing filter is used to good effect, increasing contrast in the dramatic sky. A polarizer must be used sparingly with the panoramic format, as the width of the lens will often create a darker patch of blue sky in the centre of the slide. Such problems rarely arise when the camera is used vertically.

page 26-27
Lone swan, St James's Park
June 2005; Fuji G617 105mm, Lee 0.6 ND grad, Velvia 50 asa
I'm no wildlife photographer. My patience is limited to waiting for clouds to move to where I want them. Distant shots of slow-moving swans are within my capabilities though, and when this obliging creature sailed gracefully towards Horse Guards, I was ready with a short exposure.

pages 28-29
Crescent moon at dawn, Thames
Jan 2006; Fuji G617 105mm, Lee 0.6 ND grad, Velvia 50 asa
A simple shot of the crescent moon setting against the foreground of Westminster and the Eye. Exposure times need to be kept down when photographing the moon; its motion will lead to blurring on the image if the shutter is open too long.

pages 30-31
Flower beds, Green Park gate
July 2005; Fuji G617 105mm, Velvia 50 asa
This image, sweet enough to grace a gift-box of butter toffee, was taken on a sweltering July day as excited tourists gathered for the Changing of the Guard. I was being typically contrary, preferring to focus on the angular flowerbeds and immaculate topiary outside Green Park.

pages 32-33
Westminster Abbey at night
Feb 2006; Fuji G617 105mm, Velvia 50 asa
Another bitterly cold night for a long exposure. As seems inevitable in this area, I was again approached by a policeman, this time a young chap. After the routine checks he promised to look out for my book. It was a shame we couldn't have met away from the pressures of work and in warmer conditions.

pages 34-35
Victoria Embankment, dawn
Jan 2006; Fuji G617 105mm, Lee 0.6 ND grad & polarizer, Velvia 50 asa
A winter dawn: the sun edges above hazy cloud near the horizon and illuminates the imposing mansion houses of Northumberland Avenue, bringing out detail and reflecting subtle colour in the stone. London can make such architectural masterpieces seem commonplace.

pages 36-37
Palace of Westminster and the Thames
Apr 2005; Fuji G617 105mm, Lee 0.6 ND grad, Velvia 50 asa
A bright and breezy April morning, and a simple shot from Lambeth Bridge using a graduated filter to enhance the definition of the attractive cloud features. The peaceful nature of the image belies the grinding cars and buses of the rush hour a few yards behind me.

pages 38-39
Trafalgar Square by night
Nov 2005; Fotoman 617 180mm Rodenstock, RTP 64 asa
I spent a number of hours scouting in Trafalgar Square trying to find an ideal angle, with varying degrees of success, but no ultimate satisfaction. Finally, I stepped backwards and settled on this overview, using a ground glass with the Fotoman for precise positioning of the crucial details. Simple is often best.

pages 40-41
Buckingham Palace from St James's Park
Sep 2005; Fuji G617 105mm, Lee 0.6 ND grad, Velvia 50 asa
Strong morning sunshine strikes the stonework of Buckingham Palace, from the bridge viewpoint in St James's Park. This made for a tricky exposure, given that the building was so much brighter than the other elements of the picture. To compensate for this I angled a grad down on the left to cover the Palace.

pages 42-43
Big Ben and traffic trails
Feb 2006; Fuji G617 105mm, Velvia 50 asa
I don't keep precise timings on my shots, but Big Ben helps here. A simple stylistic trick is in action: to pull the traffic trails and other diagonals into the corners of the frame. The only worry after that was to prevent pedestrians from crashing into the tripod in the darkness, as the bridge was still busy.

pages 46-47
Dying sun from Tower 42
Jan 2006; Fuji G617 105mm, Lee 0.3 & 0.9 ND grads, Velvia 50 asa
Open windows at Vertigo Bar are generally discouraged, so I was alerted to the risk of reflections from the glass. The solution was to position the lens as close to the glass as I could. Despite several unwanted layers of filtration from the window, the results were pleasing, as the winter sun fell into a dense haze.

page 48
Leadenhall Market
Apr 2005; Nikon Coolpix 5200
Evening diners enjoy a window seat above the City's historic Leadenhall Market. Meanwhile, I was left out in the cold.

page 49
Symmetry, Swiss Re
Sept 2005; Nikon Coolpix 5200
For me, the Swiss Re looks great from all angles, but I can understand why some claim it to be the right building in the wrong place. Many good sightlines towards it are blocked; perhaps the position doesn't do it justice. Here I focus on the wonderful symmetry of the design at street level.

pages 50-51
Rainbow, Tower Bridge
Apr 2005; Fuji G617 105mm, Lee 0.6 ND grad, Velvia 50 asa
Having dodged a heavy April shower in a South Bank coffee shop, I emerged just in time to view a diminishing rainbow behind Tower Bridge. Rainbows are horribly transient; seeing them fade in front of my eyes while I set up is a familiar feeling.

pages 52-53
Chinese barge, Canary Wharf
Feb 2006; Fuji G617 105mm, Lee 0.3 ND grad, Velvia 50 asa
My single shot this day proved to me once again that you shouldn't always write off grey conditions. The restaurant barge and the Canary towers juxtaposed give a sense of East meets West, Hong Kong or Singapore in miniature.

pages 54-55
Royal Victoria Dock at dawn
Jun 2005; Fuji G617 105mm, Lee 0.6 ND grad, Velvia 50 asa
Things have changed dramatically since my first visit to the Royal Victoria Dock as a teenager in 1987, but the iconic steel forms of the cranes remain exactly as they were. My exposure here was simply a question of timing as the June sun lit the new apartments on the south of the dock.

pages 56-57
Millennium Bridge at night
Nov 2005; Fotoman 617 180mm Rodenstock, RTP 64 asa
I must assume the Millennium Bridge was designed chiefly for photographers, though it makes for a handy river-crossing too. My only concern was the loss of my pen torch, meaning I had to rely on the glow from an unreliable cigarette lighter to wind on the Fotoman. I don't smoke, but I might have started just then.

pages 58-59
Swiss Re
Nov 2005; Fuji G617 105mm, Lee 0.9 ND grad, Velvia 50 asa
The gleaming spire of the Swiss Re outstrips those of the former greats of the capital's architecture that still adorn this area. Today we must thank the god of international finance for producing such monuments. If all were as imaginative and uncompromising as this one, I would have few complaints.

pages 60-61
View east from the Monument
Jun 2005; Fuji G617 105mm, Lee 0.3 ND grad, Velvia 50 asa
When the Monument was built to commemorate the Great Fire, an observer from it must have felt like a king. Today, surrounded by mundane office blocks, the view is less commanding, but remains impressive, particularly towards the Tower in the east. There's no tripod space here, so the Fuji had to be hand-held.

pages 62-63
Evening, Limehouse Basin
Jun 2005; Fuji G617 105mm, Lee 0.9 ND grad, Velvia 50 asa
While many locations were planned in advance for the project, Limehouse Basin came as a complete surprise. After randomly stepping off the Docklands Light Railway, I found inspiration in the spacious dock and fine vista towards Canary Wharf. Not a shock to locals, I'm sure, but certainly to an ignorant Northerner.

Royal Exchange, the City
Jan 2006; Fuji G617 105mm, Lee 0.6 ND grad, Velvia 50 asa
While the movers and shakers have dispersed across town, the Royal Exchange and the Bank of England still feel like the fiscal heart of the nation. This small arena proved difficult to encapsulate when standing back, so I closed in on the Corinthian columns of the Exchange, to give them back their grandeur.

St Paul's Cathedral
Apr 2005; Fuji G617 105mm, Lee 0.9 ND grad & polarizer, Velvia 50 asa
This session was quick to compose, but shooting took three long hours in total. As can happen in April, there was heavy cloud with small breaks here and there. Indeed, at one point I broke off to look for other potential subjects, but was compelled to return when the sun re-emerged.

New city from East India
Jun 2005; Fuji G617 105mm, Lee 0.9 ND grad, Velvia 50 asa
There was never any question as to whether I should photograph Canary Wharf, only where from, and the DLR stations of Blackwall and East India provided an answer. I found the opportunity late on a June evening after sundown. The unclouded afterglow proved an ideal backdrop for the dynamic lines of the foreground.

View from Tate Modern balcony
Feb 2006; Fuji G617 105mm film: RTP 64 asa
The final shoot of the project, and a chance to celebrate with friends at Tate Modern. Coffee was my drink of choice until the final roll was back in the camera bag – quite fitting, as coffee had fuelled much of the effort. Once I had positioned my diagonals and carefully judged exposure, I moved on to something more medicinal.

St Paul's from Millennium Bridge
Apr 2005; Fuji G617 105mm, Lee 0.3 ND grad & polarizer, Velvia 50 asa
Trying to time the optimum cloud position with the smallest number of bridge users was a challenge. Using a polarizer had the side effect of softening the impact of the walkers by giving them motion blur, but exposure had to be kept down to retain detail in the cloud and avoid vibration from those walking past me.

Millennium Mill, Royal Victoria Dock
Jun 2005; Fuji G617 105mm, Lee 0.6 ND grad, Velvia 50 asa
The Millennium Mill is a remarkable hulk of a building that appears to have slipped into the same planning black hole that Battersea Power Station inhabits: too good to demolish, but apparently too difficult to develop. Today it stars in TV programmes needing a backdrop of urban decay.

Canary Wharf fireworks
Nov 2005; Fuji G617 105mm, Velvia 50 asa
After a frantic chase around Rotherhithe to find a good location, I stumbled across a posse of waiting media and enthusiastic amateurs already in place. Shooting fireworks with only four frames to a roll isn't ideal, particularly fumbling in the dark to change rolls quickly and judging exposure by how many rockets have been lit.

Evening skies from Primrose Hill
Apr 2005; Fuji G617 105mm, Lee 0.6 ND grad, Velvia 50 asa
An April evening with a very chill wind and a choice of exposure time that produced an improved result. The first, at 5 seconds, left the cloud shapes intact, but was somewhat bland; the second, going up to 40 seconds, meant that the wind had time to stretch the cloud into more attractive patterns in the sky.

Leaves, Russell Square
Nov 2005; Fuji G617 105mm, Lee 81c grad & 0.6 ND grad, Velvia 50 asa
There seems no better time to shoot autumn leaves than the autumn, but even then I had to be sharp and run the gauntlet of an eager council worker raking them into huge mounds to scoop up later. When I explained my task, he kindly diverted to equally important rakings elsewhere.

Cranes, new Wembley Stadium
Feb 2006; Fuji G617 105mm, Lee 0.6 ND grad, Velvia 50 asa
One day (perhaps by the 2012 edition of this book), the new Wembley Stadium will be finished. It already looks rather magnificent, worthy of the aspirations of the country. As a fan of Sunderland AFC though, I'm not sure I'll be rushing back. My three previous visits have all coincided with personal tragedy!

Dawn colours, Little Venice
Sep 2005; Fuji G617 105mm, Lee 0.3 ND grad, Velvia 50 asa
A tranquil oasis amid flyovers and tangled railways, Little Venice shows what was achieved in a less frantic era of transport. The few sleepy barge dwellers I encountered seemed entirely at odds with the suited folk dashing to work down the towpath at Paddington.

Bandstand in winter, Regent's Park
Jan 2006; Fuji G617 105mm, Lee 81c & 0.6 ND grad, Velvia 50 asa
The news proclaimed this the 'coldest night in the capital for many years', and twin willows and the deserted bandstand reflect the mood of still hibernation in Regent's Park. A warm-up filter was employed to balance the blue caste that often comes from Velvia in this lighting, but it did little to warm up the frozen photographer.

Gary climbs The Writer, Parliament Hill
Jul 2005; Fuji G617 105mm, Lee 0.6 ND grad, Velvia 50 asa
Alerted to the commotion at the table and chair, which I was composing from a distance, I closed in to find Gary shinning up the chair leg and delighting all onlookers except his horrified girlfriend (seen as a white blur). With only RVP50 in the camera, cutting the exposure time to the bone was still not enough.

Colonnade, Regent's Crescent
Jan 2006; Nikon Coolpix 5200
The perfectly ordered Georgian columns of Park Crescent glow in the winter sunlight.

BT Tower
Jan 2006; Nikon Coolpix 5200
It seemed sensible to shoot the BT Tower (formerly the Post Office tower) in a vertical format; though finding the perfect vantage point was no easy task.

pages 94-95

BT Tower from Regent's Park

Feb 2006; Fotoman 617 180mm Rodenstock,
Lee 0.6 ND grad & polarizer, Velvia 50 asa

Hazy sunlight did little to warm Regent's Park on this cold afternoon and the light mist made the distant view of the BT Tower indistinct. I found that by using a polarizer in conjunction with a two-stop grad (angled to cover the top right-hand corner) I could give the tower its true importance and clarity.

pages 96-97

Summer, Hampstead Heath

Jul 2005; Fuji G617 105mm, Lee 0.3 ND grad &
polarizer, Velvia 50 asa

The view from Parliament Hill, on a hot July afternoon. The dried grass is indicative of the lack of rainfall in the south of England, a problem that could possibly get much worse. During my stays in the capital there were of course showers, but I was never put out of action by prolonged rain.

pages 98-99

Kenwood House, Hampstead Heath

Jun 2005; Fuji G617 105mm, Lee 0.6 ND grad &
polarizer, Velvia 50 asa

Kenwood House presides over the northern end of Hampstead Heath and is more normally photographed from the south. However, on a late June evening the sun has moved around to bathe the northern façade with light. A polarizer toned down the most powerful reflections from the buildings.

pages 100-101

Lamps, Alexandra Palace

Sep 2005; Fuji G617 105mm unfiltered, Velvia 50
asa

I did not, of course, travel to Alexandra Palace with the intention of avoiding images of the building, but under ominous skies there was no light cast on it. Instead, I was unable to resist the dramas occurring in the skies to the south as a thunderstorm crossed Highgate and headed north-west.

pages 102-103

Autumn, Tavistock Square

Oct 2005; Fuji G617 105mm, Lee 81c, Velvia 50 asa

A trip to Tavistock Square was a pilgrimage to pay my respects to those who died on 7 July. I found that the scene was one of peaceful normality, with office workers enjoying their lunches and reading newspapers. Only the quickening breeze and buildings shrouded in plastic gave a reminder of the disturbing events three months previously.

pages 104-105

BT Tower from Capper Street

Jan 2006; Fuji G617 105mm unfiltered,
Velvia 50 asa

Here I elected to shoot the BT Tower from Fitzroy Square, using the convergence of the Fuji lens as a feature to bring together the gable ends of the buildings on Conway Street. The set-up had to be speedy and portable, as the best position proved to be in the middle of the road.

pages 106-107

Swans, Hampstead Heath

Jul 2005; Fuji G617 105mm, Lee 0.6 ND grad,
Velvia 50 asa

A summer evening on one of the Highgate ponds, and a pair of swans go about their business in a relaxed fashion. Hampstead Heath is the stamping ground of Bill Oddie, and it would have surprised me little to run into him, binoculars in hand, taking in the balmy evening air.

pages 108-109

Cracked ice, Regent's Park

Jan 2006; Fuji G617 105mm, Lee 81c,
Velvia 50 asa

There were few takers for the pedalos on this bitter morning in Regent's Park – an icebreaker would have been more appropriate. In trying to include the foreground ice, I pushed the G617 to its limit (it isn't keen on close-focusing) and used f45 for as much depth of field as I could muster.

pages 112-113

View west, Park Lane Hilton

Nov 2005; Fuji G617 105mm, Lee 0.9 ND grad,
Velvia 50 asa

With only two afternoons to capture the view from the Park Lane Hilton, it was going to require a little good fortune to gain workable conditions. The first evening was flat and grey. The second, however, brought a sublime fading sunset, which was surprisingly well defined by a heavy graduated filter.

pages 114-115

Stream, Richmond Park

Nov 2005; Fotoman 617 180mm Rodenstock,
Lee 0.9 ND grad, Velvia 50 asa

This view on a small footbridge near Pen Ponds had many themes I look for in a panorama: strong lead-in lines, a distinct central feature, good symmetry and nice light to boot. To ensure the utmost accuracy, I used the Fotoman and ground glass, and positioned the central tree precisely.

pages 116-117

Fluffy cloud, Hampton Court Palace

Jan 2006; Fuji G617 105mm, Lee 0.6 ND grad,
Velvia 50 asa

Richmond photographer Joanna Jackson was an invaluable guide to Hampton Court Palace and its grounds. As I prepared another all-encompassing panorama, she was happily rummaging in the undergrowth somewhere. (She prefers to focus on details!)

pages 118-119

Leaf shower, Kew

Nov 2005; Fuji G617 105mm unfiltered,
Velvia 50 asa

A rather experimental moment (I have to remind myself to experiment more often) in Kew Gardens under the canopy of an autumnal tree. This was a sparkling November afternoon, and my heart was warmed by the opportunities for shooting, as well as by the friendly staff at Kew who went out of their way to be helpful.

pages 120-121

Houseboats, Kew Bridge

Sep 2005; Fuji G617 105mm, Lee 0.6 ND grad &
81c, Velvia 50 asa

Floating homes line the river at various points between here and Chelsea, and give respite from traffic noise, as well as being safe from the long-term threat of increased flooding. At low tide the green algae in the river is revealed, and by the time shooting was over I was covered in mud.

pages 122-123

Serpentine sunset, Hyde Park

Sep 2005; Fuji G617 105mm, Lee 0.3 ND grad,
Velvia 50 asa

A gaudy September sunset in Hyde Park, captured from the eastern end of the Serpentine. I don't go seeking out glorious sunsets, and when they come another point of interest such as a striking silhouette is advantageous. However, this one seemed to continually intensify in colour, before eventually fading.

pages 124-125

Temple, Kew Gardens

Nov 2005; Fuji G617 105mm, Lee 0.9 ND grad,
Velvia 50 asa

Firing into the sun is a hit-and-miss practice at the best of times, and when you're trying to retain foreground detail it is especially difficult. Here, shooting at Kew, I just about got away with it, avoiding damaging flare (another problem with such a wide lens) by a whisker.

The superb brick mansions of Kensington Gore were an obvious subject, but I thought that trying to shoot in full sunlight would have caused too many deep shadows. Instead, I chose to shoot under flat grey skies, but problems still remained with the parked cars, so I had to extend my tripod to its full two-metre height.

There are always opportunities for shooting with fast-moving fluffy cumulus, and, after I discovered Ham House to be covered in scaffolding, Marble Hill House on the opposite bank provided a good setting. I was rewarded with a life-saving cup of tea and selection of cream cakes by the wonderful staff at Ham House.

I came to the Albert Bridge late on an evening in high summer, and waited for what seemed like an age for the bulbs to illuminate. Finally I looked down to check my exposure, looked up again and the bridge was lit, with pallid blue cloud in the background. The timing and light came together perfectly.

Autumn is always my favourite time to shoot, but I was taken by surprise by this magnificent horse-chestnut on the Thames Path near Chiswick. This was early September and the tree seemed to be making premature contingency plans for winter.

I intended to shoot the Palm House head-on, and did indeed enjoy success from that angle, but the best of the cloud was to the north. To give better balance, I decamped to the corner of the greenhouse, where I also found shadows stretching across the lawn adding further drama to the image.

The Albert Memorial was a classic subject for a panoramic camera, but this proved a difficult location in which to gauge exposure, thanks to the small gap of light between the trees and the dazzling sunlight on the gilded statue. Filtration had to be a compromise between toning down the sky and keeping the trees from darkness.

At the end of a beautiful November afternoon, the falling sun brings intense colour to the lake and surrounding trees, while gulls pose dutifully for their portrait. Adding to the colour are the floating globules of Chihuly glass and the extravagant rowing boat commandeered by the sculptor.

The Royal Albert Hall required some thought over timing and conditions, given its rather cramped location. The steps and forecourt were occupied by extras from a feature film on location at the Science Museum behind me. Little did they know they would appear on celluloid twice in one day.

Intense greens of late spring give a lush appearance to the Italianate gardens of Kensington Palace in Hyde Park. The magnificent gilded gates of the palace were obscured by hundreds of personal memorials to Lady Diana, which made for its own panorama.

Walking into Richmond Park at dawn for the first time was a revelation, despite having read enough to know a little of what to expect. A lone stag grazed 50 metres to the left of shot, but I knew my lenses would not allow me to pick it up in detail, and stalking is not one of my specialities.

I had heard that this particular view from Henry VIII's mound in Richmond was 'the most painted view in England'. It was a claim I was not able to verify, but it may be equally difficult to disprove. The new Wembley arch, far to the north-west, is barely a dot on the horizon.

A blustery and occasionally wet April day, but ideal for shooting. The Eye is universally accepted as part of the London skyline, and even slipped unopposed into the protected view from the bridge in St James's Park. Here, from the Embankment, it towers over County Hall, former seat of power of the Greater London Council.

After a frustrating hour of scouting I found myself running down Nine Elms Lane, to catch a vivid red sky behind the world's most famous chimneys. I finally stopped outside a busy pub and found a pleasing silhouette. Strange that the derelict industrial hulk of Battersea Power Station should provoke such admiration.

To another hefty white elephant on the other side of town, which again I can only admire. I appreciate the Dome for what it is now, a quite beautiful folly that catches the light delightfully at dawn in June. I mused whether a polarizer added or detracted, and on this occasion was happier with the non-polarized version.

Strolling downhill in Greenwich Park I had one of those moments that you long for in this line of work: sighting the distant Docklands towers perfectly framed by a gap in the trees. The brisk breeze was the only concern, and I elected to use it as a feature, extending the exposure to three seconds with a polarizer.

page 158
National Theatre at night
Jan 2006; Nikon Coolpix 5200
The changing colours of the floodlights of the National Theatre add an enticing note of interest to a building that has had its fair share of critics, but now seems a stable icon on the South Bank.

pages 159
Lamp and London Eye
Jan 2006; Nikon Coolpix 5200
The London Eye towers over the South Bank's iconic lanterns on a frosty morning in January.

pages 160-161
Greenwich Yacht Club
Sep 2005; Fuji G617 105mm, Lee 0.6 ND grad, Velvia 50 asa
Intending to shoot the Thames Barrier, I was enjoying a pleasant if somewhat odorous walk down the Thames Path from the Dome, when I discovered the curious building on stilts: the Greenwich Yacht Club. Using a nearby building to narrowly shield myself from the sun, I balanced the blues of sky and river with a ND grad.

pages 162-163
Television mast, Crystal Palace
Nov 2005; Fuji G617 105mm, Lee 0.6 ND grad & polarizer, Velvia 50 asa
Perhaps not a romantic choice, but, given its visibility as a landmark from right across the capital I felt the TV mast of Crystal Palace deserved an appearance, particularly as I was able to capture it in delicious autumn light. An angled grad was used to hold the sky, while avoiding contact with the line of trees.

pages 164-165
Fireworks in Battersea Park
Nov 2005; Fotoman 617 180mm Rodenstock unfiltered, Velvia 100f
The 400th anniversary of Guy Fawkes' attempt to blow up the Houses of Parliament is celebrated with fireworks. These days he would struggle to take a photograph of the building, never mind lace it with gunpowder. I was at the safe distance of a flat in Chelsea, where I had gatecrashed a party to capture this exposure.

pages 166-167
Royal Naval College, Greenwich
Apr 2005; Fuji G617 105mm, Lee 0.3 ND grad, Velvia 50 asa
Long one of my favourite buildings in London, the Royal Naval College posed the problem of where to shoot from. The answer was to approach from the bank of the Thames. Pale sunlight avoided dense shadows and there was just about enough in the sky to give a further point of reference.

pages 168-169
Dinosaur lake, Crystal Palace Park
Nov 2005; Fotoman G617 180mm Rodenstock, Lee 81ef, Velvia 50 asa
I've always found the Crystal Palace dinosaurs to be cute rather than scary. Pedantic complaints have persisted that the designs fail to follow the fossil record with any accuracy – but I can't help imagining that this chap once strode out in south London and chewed on passing photographers.

pages 170-171
Fiery dawn, Jubilee Bridge
Jan 2006; Fuji G617 105mm, Lee 0.6 ND grad, Velvia 50 asa
A fiercely burning dawn sky, shot from the western Jubilee Bridge. Frosting on the pavement gives an indication of the temperature of the morning. A medium ND grad was needed to balance the sky and foreground; I took readings from the brightest sky and the highlighted railing.

pages 172-173
The Paragon, Blackheath
Nov 2005; Fotoman 617 180mm Rodenstock, Lee 0.3 ND grad & polarizer, Velvia 50 asa
A short walk from Greenwich Park is the Paragon at Blackheath. Quite why all houses weren't made this way, I've no idea. The only thing liable to spoil the scene was the row of cars, so I took a low vantage point behind a grass verge to lessen their impact.

pages 174-175
Dawn from Waterloo Bridge
Jan 2006; Fuji G617 105mm, Lee 0.6 ND grad, Velvia 50 asa
The January rising sun highlights strange linear forms in the cloud, and steam rises from the vents of various buildings, as if they are stirring from slumber. Curiously, Waterloo was probably the only accessible bridge I'd not crossed by this time, and I had to be tipped off that the views from here could be special.

pages 176-177
Cloud banks from Greenwich Park
Nov 2005; Fuji G617 105mm, Lee 0.9 ND grad, Velvia 50 asa
I'd visited this spot twice before at dawn, and the best I'd come up with was a bland blue sky, so I was delighted to see such interesting cloud forms from the Observatory hill. Two separate weather systems seemed to be meeting for my benefit, and although the sunlight was intermittent and weak, there was just enough.

pages 178-179
Looking east, London Eye
Feb 2006; Fuji G617 105mm, Lee 0.6 ND grad Provia 400 asa
The London Eye was conceived and designed by Marks Barfield Architects. The wheel is constantly moving, so my usual 50 asa film had to be replaced with Provia 400. A combination of polarization and getting as close to the glass as possible was the best compromise I could find.

pages 180-181
Cutty Sark, spring morning
Apr 2005; Fuji G617 105mm, Lee 0.3 ND grad & polarizer, Velvia 50 asa
Bright sunlight strikes the venerable timbers of the *Cutty Sark*, on a pristine morning in April. Using diagonals, here formed by the ship and the trees on the right, is a classic technique in all formats of landscape photography, but in the panoramic format is particularly important.

pages 182-183
Christmas lights, South Bank
Jan 2006; Fotoman 617 180mm Rodenstock unfiltered, RTP 64 asa
I often think of myself as somewhat lucky with the conditions I find, but this particular stroke of luck owed nothing to the weather. Finding these Christmas lights still switched on in late January made for a wonderful foreground for a vista of St Paul's.

ACKNOWLEDGEMENTS

Mark Denton would like to thank the following who have helped directly in the making of this book:

Patrick Bongartz, Jen Brown at London Eye, Victoria Brown, Joe Cornish, Mike Denton, Rachel Denton, Pete Duncan at Constable, Paul Droluk at Fotoman, staff at Ham House, Bob Harvey, Eryl Humphrey Jones at Constable, Joanna Jackson, Delme Jenkins, Liz Johnston, staff at Kew Gardens, Edgar King at Trinity House, Helena Lundberg at Hilton Park Lane, Anne Maidment, Margaret at NPS Media, Graham Merritt at Lee Filters, Anthony Mortimer, Dick and Steve at Positive Images, Colin Prior, John Rendall, Ian & Tina Semple, Richard Stott, staff at Tate Modern, Virginie Van Hoecke at Vertigo, Steven Wignill.

Mapping on pages 184-185 (© ML Design 2006) based originally on the 1939 Bartholomew Atlas, revised with the assistance of copyright free material provided by Alan Collinson Design and checked extensively on foot. Subsequent revisions courtesy of Lovell Johns Ltd, Oxford and David Haslam Publishing, Glos.

Mark Denton recommends Lee Filters (www.leefilters.co.uk). Film processing was by NPS Media, Middlesbrough (www.npsmedia.com) and Positive Images, Richmond on Thames (www.positive-images.co.uk)

Mark Denton's images are distributed by Panoramic Images, Inc. (Chicago) at www.panoramicimages.com and by www.markdentonphotographic.co.uk. Some images are used with kind permission of Panoramic Images, Inc.

Limited edition prints of images from this book are available from www.markdentonphotographic.co.uk

For prints, postcards, commissions, photo sales and any other enquiries see www.markdentonphotographic.co.uk or contact Mark at markdentonphotographic@yahoo.co.uk and on 07709 905639.